Healing through the Creator's Eyes

A Scripture-Based Guide to Self-Love & Wholeness

A work of love by Gordon R.L. Hikel II, inspired by the Scriptures.

"You are worthy, Jehovah our God, to receive the glory and the honor and the power, because you created all things, and because of your will they came into existence and were created."
— Revelation 4:11, NWT

Copyright © 2025 Gordon R.L Hikel II.
All Rights Reserved.

No part of this publication may be reproduced, stored in a retrieval system, or transmitted in any form or by any means—electronic, mechanical, photocopy, recording, or otherwise—without the prior written permission of the author.

Unless otherwise indicated, all Scriptures are quoted from the *New World Translation of the Holy Scriptures,* published by Watch Tower Bible and Tract Society of Pennsylvania.

This book is a work of encouragement and spiritual reflection. It is not affiliated with or endorsed by any religious organization.

Written by Gordon R.L Hikel II

Published by Gordon R.L Hikel II

Dedication

"Come to me, all you who are toiling and loaded down, and I will refresh you. Take my yoke upon you and learn from me, for I am mild-tempered and lowly in heart, and you will find refreshment for yourselves. For my yoke is kindly, and my load is light."

— Matthew 11:28–30, NWT

These tender words were spoken by Jesus Christ, the Son of God, who looked upon the crowds—tired, weary, and lost—and "he felt deep compassion for them, because they were skinned and thrown about like sheep without a shepherd."

— Matthew 9:36, NWT ("compassion" used in place of "pity" for clarity)

He spoke not on His own authority, but in full and perfect unity with His Father, who entrusted Him with all authority in heaven and on earth Matthew 28:18. It was through this divine commission that Jesus extended this loving invitation—an invitation still open to every soul today.

This book is dedicated to

the lost, the weary, the brokenhearted,

the overlooked and overwhelmed,

the fatherless, and those who feel forgotten.

To all who carry invisible burdens,

and to those who long for peace but don't know where to find it.

May you hear the voice of Jesus calling gently,

"Come to me…"

May your heart find rest in His kindness,

and may His love lift your spirit, restore your hope,

and remind you that you are never alone.

You are seen.

You are loved.

You matter.

Table of Contents

Introduction   1

Chapter 1: Created with Purpose   3

Chapter 2: Wonderfully Made   5

Chapter 3: Never Alone   7

Chapter 4: You Are Empowered Beyond Measure   9

Chapter 5: You Are Renewed in the Waiting   11

Chapter 6: You Are Strengthened to Endure with Joy   13

Chapter 7: Strength in Weakness   15

Chapter 8: You Are Seen and Remembered – Even When Others Forget   16

Chapter 9: You Are Gifted with Purpose   18

Chapter 10: You Are Capable of the Impossible   20

Chapter 11: The Unfathomable Love That Restores and Blesses   22

Chapter 12: You Are a Light to the World   25

Chapter 13: Unshakably Loved — 27

Chapter 14: You Are Being Restored and Made Strong — 29

Chapter 15: You Are Held by a Hopeful Future — 31

Chapter 16: You Are Made to Reflect His Qualities — 33

Chapter 17: Righteous in God's Eyes — 35

Chapter 18: Empowered for Good — 36

Chapter 19: Forgive and Be Free —the Doorway to Healing Opens through Forgiveness — 38

Chapter 20: The Journey of Return – Repentance and the Beauty of a Renewed Mind — 40

Conclusion — **42**

Acknowledgments — **43**

Introduction

This book is a powerful guide designed to help you experience healing by seeing yourself through the eyes of your Creator. Each page walks you through carefully chosen Scriptures that reveal your value, identity, and potential.

If you are struggling with a lack of self-love, guilt, or even self doubt, this book leads you back to The Truth: you come from love and that you are loved, seen, and wonderfully made with a divine purpose.

For each verse, you'll find:

Truth:

A clear explanation of what the scripture reveals about you.

Reflect:

An encouraging message to stir your heart and shift your mindset.

Affirmation:

A declaration to speak over yourself and embrace.

May these pages help you see yourself not through fear, shame, or judgment, but through the Creator's eyes—eyes full of love, purpose, and power.

Chapter 1

Created with Purpose

Genesis 1:31 "God saw everything he had made, and look! it was very good."

Truth:

You were created with intention and love. Everything about you was designed to be good in God's eyes, regardless of others' judgments or your past mistakes.

Reflect:

Consider this: The Creator of the universe looked at you—your heart, personality, being—and declared it very good. Not just acceptable, but very good. Despite what others say or mistakes you've made, the Creator still sees you as very good. You are not defined by your past, labels, or failures. You are a reflection of divine purpose, shaped by love and intention. Embrace this truth—God sees you as a beautiful creation, and His view matters most.

Affirmation:

I am a beautiful creation of God, and He sees me as very good.

Chapter 2

Wonderfully Made

Psalm 139:14 "I praise you because in an awe-inspiring way I am wonderfully made. Your works are wonderful, I know this very well."

Truth:

You are a masterpiece of divine craftsmanship, made with awe-inspiring detail and beauty.

Reflect:

You are wonderfully made—not just in idea, but in real, tangible, undeniable ways. When you get a cut, your body begins to heal. Around the world, people are rising above physical challenges—running marathons with prosthetic legs, and lifting weights without the full use or presence of their arms, demonstrating incredible strength through their core, legs, and creative adaptations. These stories aren't about limitation—they are living proof of the extraordinary resilience, adaptability, and brilliance built into us all. You are living proof of design and purpose. You were not thrown together; you were intricately woven with care. No matter what you've been through, the Creator's craftsmanship in you remains. You are capable, adaptive, strong—and yes, still wonderfully made.

Affirmation:

I am wonderfully made. My body, mind, and spirit carry divine design. Even when life challenges me, I rise, heal, and overcome. I am living proof of the Creator's greatness.

Chapter 3

Never Alone

Deuteronomy 31:6 "Be courageous and strong… Jehovah your God is the one marching with you. He will neither desert you nor abandon you."

Truth:

You are never alone—Jehovah walks with you through every season.

Reflect:

In the darkest valley or on the brightest mountaintop, you are never alone. You are surrounded by unshakable love. The One who formed the stars walks beside you with intentional care and relentless strength. Even when silence echoes, you are seen, known, and cherished. His presence is a present reality. He is your refuge, anchor, and strength. Trust that every step is guided, every tear noticed, and every prayer heard. You are never forsaken but profoundly loved.

Affirmation:

I am never alone—Jehovah is always with me.

Chapter 4

You Are Empowered Beyond Measure

Philippians 4:13 "For all things I have the strength through the one who gives me power."

Truth:

Your strength doesn't depend on your resources—it flows from the Creator. His spirit empowers you to overcome, endure, and thrive.

Reflect:

There will be times when your strength runs low. But you were never meant to carry it all alone. The power fueling your soul is divine, unshakable, and abundant. When you feel like you've reached your end, divine strength begins. Look upward, not inward. Trust that you are filled with a power greater than anything you face. You can rise, rebuild, and press forward because you are never without the One who strengthens you. His power is your source.

Affirmation:

I am strong in God. His power flows through me, and I can do all things through Him.

Chapter 5

You Are Renewed in the Waiting

Isaiah 40:29–31 "He gives power to the tired one... Those hoping in Jehovah will regain power. They will soar on wings like eagles."

Truth:

Jehovah renews the strength of those who trust in Him, especially when they feel weak or weary.

Reflect:

Life drains us. But the promise of renewal is rooted in your hope. When you trust in Jehovah, you're being restored. You are like an eagle, made to soar. Even when you feel empty, His strength is being poured into you. Rest is sacred. In stillness, you are lifted. In quiet hope, you are empowered. Dare to believe that your low moments are not the end, but the beginning of your rise?

Affirmation:

Jehovah renews my strength. I rise like an eagle, strong and full of hope.

Chapter 6

You Are Strengthened to Endure with Joy

Colossians 1:11 "And may you be strengthened with all power according to his glorious might so that you may endure fully with patience and joy."

Truth:

God strengthens you and fills you with patience and joy as you endure life's challenges.

Reflect:

Endurance isn't just surviving—it's growing stronger, deeper, and more joyful. You were designed to walk through storms with an unshaken spirit. The power you draw from the Creator is vibrant, full of glory, and infused with joy. Even in difficulty, you are never alone, empty, or without purpose. His strength is constant, and His joy is your hidden reservoir. Patience becomes your peace, and joy becomes your anthem. What if today, you invited joy to walk with you?

Affirmation:

I am empowered by God to endure with joy and patience.

Chapter 7

Strength in Weakness

2 Corinthians 12:9 "My undeserved kindness is sufficient for you, for my power is being made perfect in weakness."

Truth:

Your weaknesses are where God's power shines the most.

Reflect:

You don't need to be flawless to be filled with divine power. In your weakest places, God leans in close. His kindness covers your struggle, and His strength lifts your spirit. You are not defined by failure but empowered by undeserved kindness, mercy, grace.

Affirmation:

God's strength is made perfect in me, even in my weakness.

Chapter 8

You Are Seen and Remembered – Even When Others Forget

Psalm 27:10 "Though my own father and mother may leave me, Jehovah himself will take me in."

Truth:

Human love isn't always consistent. People may walk away. Family may fail to understand. But Jehovah never forgets you. He remains, sees you, values you, and chooses you—always.

Reflect:

You are never invisible to Jehovah. Even if those closest leave, ignore your pain, or fail to see your light, Jehovah does. He knows your heart, hears every cry, and sees every tear. His love isn't based on performance but on your worth, which He gave you. When the world turns its back, Jehovah opens His arms. When you feel forgotten, He whispers your name. You are remembered with divine care and held in the deepest love. There is no rejection so painful that His acceptance cannot heal. You are His beloved child, and He will never leave you behind.

Affirmation:

Even if others forget me, Jehovah remembers me. I am fully seen, deeply loved, and forever held in His care.

Chapter 9

You Are Gifted with Purpose

Romans 12:6 "Since, then, we have gifts that differ according to the undeserved kindness given to us, let us use them."

Truth:

You have been given unique gifts by your Creator. Your purpose is to use them—not to compare or hide them.

Reflect:

Within you lies a treasure chest of gifts, placed there with care and intention. These gifts fulfill a divine purpose that only you can accomplish. You are already equipped. Don't bury your talents beneath doubt or comparison. Let them rise and shine. You were never meant to hide what was divinely placed within you. The world needs your voice, kindness, and strength—expressed uniquely.

Affirmation:

My gifts are from God the Creator. I use them boldly and joyfully.

Chapter 10

You Are Capable of the Impossible

Genesis 11:6 "Now there is nothing that they may have in mind to do that will be impossible for them."

Truth:

God acknowledged the unstoppable power of unified, focused human intention. When you rely on Him and align your mind and heart with divine truth, what once seemed impossible becomes possible.

Reflect:

You were created with potential, not limits. Even your Creator acknowledged the power within focused human effort. When your thoughts, faith, and purpose move in harmony, you become a vessel of limitless possibility. Mountains move. What was once unimaginable becomes reality. Don't shrink back in fear. If your heart aligns with divine truth and you follow Christ's example (1 Peter

2:21), the impossible is waiting for you to believe.

Affirmation:

By listening, obeying, and having faith, I will be blessed. I can accomplish what I was created for. Nothing aligned with God's will is impossible for me.

Chapter 11

The Unfathomable Love That Restores and Blesses

Scripture:

"For God loved the world so much that he gave his only-begotten Son, so that everyone exercising faith in him might not be destroyed but have everlasting life."— John 3:16 (NWT)

Truth:

You are so deeply loved by God that He gave the most precious gift imaginable—His only-begotten Son—for you. This love is not distant or generic. It is personal, intentional, and directed straight at your heart.

Reflect:

Let this truth reach deep into your soul: You were worth the greatest act of love ever shown. God saw the disconnect—the damaged relationship between Himself and humanity—and knew what needed to be done. Out of immeasurable love, He gave His Son—not only to pay a price, but to make restoration and everlasting life possible for all who exercise faith in Him. Jesus accepted that mission fully. He didn't stumble into it or simply follow a path—He chose it. With clarity, courage, and love, He took on the responsibility of bringing you back to hope. And when He thought of you, He was not burdened or reluctant—He was deeply moved. As Proverbs 8:31 says, "***I was rejoicing over the productive land, and the things I was fondest of were the sons of men***."

From the beginning, His heart was inclined with joy toward humanity. He saw you with fondness, not frustration—with delight, not disappointment. His sacrifice was not vague or mechanical; it was deliberate, deeply loving, and joyfully undertaken to bring you into the full blessing of life with God. His open arms made a way for you to be healed and made whole.

This gift is not about deserving—it is about exercising faith. Faith in the One who gave everything for you. You are not invisible. You are not beyond reach. You are deeply valued, richly blessed, and forever invited into the everlasting life His Father lovingly provides for you through exercising faith in His Son.

Affirmation:

God gave His Son for me because I am deeply loved. Christ took on the mission to bring me healing, wholeness, and the hope of everlasting life. He was glad to do it, because when He saw me, He saw someone worth loving and rejoicing over. I live each day knowing I am valued and richly blessed by the life His Father lovingly provides.

Chapter 12

You Are a Light to the World

Matthew 5:14 "You are the light of the world. A city cannot be hid when located on a mountain."

Truth:

You were created to shine. Your life has power to bring light and hope to others.

Reflect:

There is a radiant light within you that was never meant to be hidden. The world needs what you carry—the warmth of your words, the spark of your presence, the glow of your truth. You are like a city on a hill: unmistakable and filled with purpose. Don't dim your light for fear or shame. You were designed to shine boldly.

Affirmation:

I am a light in this world—bold, bright, and full of purpose.

Chapter 13

Unshakably Loved

Romans 8:38-39 "I am convinced that neither death nor life... nor anything else in creation will be able to separate us from God's love."

Truth:

Nothing can separate you from God's love.

Reflect:

His love is not fragile. It doesn't crack or fade. It is unshakable—anchored in eternity and immovable. It is not based on performance. His love sees through every layer and chooses you still. There's no distance too far, no mistake too deep—His love reaches you always. It pursues you relentlessly, embraces you completely, and heals you tenderly. Even when you feel undeserving, He calls you worthy. You are held by a love that will never let go, as long as you don't let go or abandon Him.

Affirmation:

Nothing can separate me from the love of God.

Chapter 14

You Are Being Restored and Made Strong

1 Peter 5:10 "But after you have suffered a little while, the God of all undeserved kindness, who called you to his everlasting glory in union with Christ, will himself finish your training. He will make you firm, he will make you strong, he will firmly ground you."

Truth:

Your pain is not the end of your story. God is committed to restoring you, strengthening you, and grounding you in lasting glory.

Reflect:

Even in the hardest seasons, you are never being broken without purpose. What feels like loss is often preparation. God sees your suffering and has already written restoration into your story. He lifts you with greater power, deeper roots, and renewed purpose. Trust that you are being completed.

Affirmation:

God is restoring me. He is making me strong, firm, and deeply grounded in His love.

Chapter 15

You Are Held by a Hopeful Future

Jeremiah 29:11 "'For I well know the thoughts that I am thinking toward you,' declares Jehovah, 'thoughts of peace, and not of calamity, to give you a future and a hope.'"

Truth:

Jehovah's plans for you are filled with peace, hope, and a secure future.

Reflect:

Life presents us with uncertainty. Yet, in the midst of unknowns, there is assurance. Even when you can't see the whole picture, trust that Jehovah is guiding you toward something good. Every step is part of the journey to your purpose. Trust the unfolding path, for He sees the end from the beginning. You are not walking alone; He is preparing a future for you.

Affirmation:

Jehovah's purpose for me are good. I have hope and a future in Him.

Chapter 16

You Are Made to Reflect His Qualities

Genesis 1:27 "And God went on to create the man in his image, in God's image he created him; male and female he created them."

Truth:

You were made in the image of the Creator. Your existence reflects His nature, and you are called to reflect His personality and qualities.

Reflect:

You are meant to display His character. The love, kindness, patience, and creativity you show are qualities that God embodies. In every act of compassion, you mirror His heart. You have the capacity to reflect the Creator's personality. The way you live and interact with others is an invitation for the world to see God's nature through you.

Affirmation:

I am made in the image of the Creator—I have the ability to reflect His outstanding attributes and qualities.

Chapter 17

Righteous in God's Eyes

Proverbs 24:16 "For though the righteous one may fall seven times, he will get up again…"

Truth:

What makes you righteous is not that you never fall—but that you keep getting back up, desiring to do what's right.

Reflect:

We all stumble. But the Creator doesn't define you by your falls—He looks at your willingness to rise. Each time you try again with a sincere heart, you reflect what God values: perseverance, humility, and trust in His mercy. Mistakes don't disqualify you. What matters is your response. The righteous are persistent. And every time you rise, heaven rejoices.

Affirmation:

Even if I fall, I will rise again. My sincerity and determination make me righteous in God's eyes.

Chapter 18

Empowered for Good

2 Timothy 1:7 – "For God did not give us a spirit of cowardice, but one of power and of love and of soundness of mind."

Truth:

You were not created to be ruled by fear but designed with power, anchored in love, and gifted with the ability to think clearly. The spirit within you is strong and divinely intentional.

Reflect:

Fear whispers that you're not enough. But that voice is not from the One who made you. You were given a spirit infused with power, radiating love, and grounded in calm clarity. This spirit stands with quiet confidence. You are not a mistake. The power within you can overcome, the love within you can heal, and the clarity of your mind can guide you. When you feel overwhelmed, return to this truth: you have been equipped with purpose. Step forward boldly. You were made to.

Affirmation:

I carry the spirit of power, love, and soundness of mind. I am not afraid. I am strong, clear, and full of purpose.

Chapter 19

Forgive and Be Free —the Doorway to Healing Opens through Forgiveness

Luke 11:4 "And forgive us our sins, for we ourselves also forgive everyone who is in debt to us."

Truth:

Forgiveness is something we release. The Creator designed forgiveness as a two-way flow. When you forgive others, you create space for your own healing. Forgiveness is spiritual strength that restores peace.

Reflect:

Forgiveness is a divine key. It unlocks chains and breaks cycles. When you forgive, you open your heart to receive forgiveness that only the Creator can give. He waits to pour it out. Your willingness to release offense clears the way for Him to reach deeper. It means choosing peace over poison. Every time you forgive, you declare that the past no longer holds you. The power of forgiveness covers it all. Let it flow, heal, and free you.

Affirmation:

I choose to forgive myself and others no matter the offense and in doing so, I open myself to healing. I am free from bitterness, washed in grace, and forgiven completely.

Chapter 20

The Journey of Return – Repentance and the Beauty of a Renewed Mind

Acts 3:19 "Repent, therefore, and turn around so as to get your sins blotted out, so that seasons of refreshing may come from Jehovah himself."

Truth:

Repentance is a shift of the heart and mind, a change of direction. It is turning away from what harms you and returning to what restores you. It is a movement toward healing and alignment.

Reflect:

You are not stuck in who you were. Every breath is a chance to begin again. Jehovah desires transformation. Repentance is about awakening. It's realizing the path you've walked no longer serves you and choosing a better way. It's a journey back to truth. As you turn, your mindset shifts. You see yourself through the eyes of possibility. This process is beautiful. In every sincere turn, you are met with open arms. Jehovah celebrates your return. Let His mercy guide you.

Affirmation:

I am turning toward healing and walking in truth. I am not defined by my past—I am transformed by love.

Conclusion

You are not who the world says you are, but who the Creator says you are. You are wonderfully made, seen and known, and deeply cherished. Let every truth remind you of your worth, every reflection open your heart, and every affirmation be a declaration of who you truly are. This is your journey back to seeing yourself through the Creator's eyes—with love, purpose, and power.

Acknowledgments

I give special thanks to Jah my Heavenly Father, for raising me; to my wife, Johanne Hikel, for her endless love, support, and belief in me; to our two beautiful children, who inspire me every day; to my mother, Lynette Parkinson, for her unconditional love; and to Mr. Zubair for his kind assistance with formatting.

Each of you has played a part in this journey, and I am forever grateful.

www.ingramcontent.com/pod-product-compliance
Lightning Source LLC
Chambersburg PA
CBHW032100150426
43194CB00006B/601